Fields of Dreams

by

Kenneth A. Walsh and Barbara Rogers Jolovitz

"Only those who step up to the plate can find out how far they can hit the ball."
— George Herman "Babe" Ruth, Jr.

Fields of Dreams

Copyright © 2017 by Kenneth A. Walsh and Barbara Rogers Jolovitz
All rights reserved. No part of this book may be reproduced or transmitted in any form or by any means without written permission of the author.

ISBN 978-1-943424-20-7
Library of Congress Control Number 2017936256

Cover photos: Maine's Fenway–185 miles north of Boston Red Sox Fenway Park
                  Purnell Wrigley Field–1160 miles east of Chicago's Wrigley Field

Dedicated to all the volunteers who make the GAME great.

Introduction

It's the seventh inning stretch in Chicago at Wrigley Field. Chicago Cubs fans stand as one and in one voice sing "Take Me Out to the Ball Game." It's the middle of the eighth in Boston at Fenway Park. Red Sox fans are on their feet. "Sweet Caroline" in one voice lets you know the Sox are home.

These two baseball parks are coming together in central Maine. They share similar histories, the first being that they are the first and second oldest ballparks in the majors. Fenway Park was built in 1912 and Wrigley Park in 1914; both have unique outfields. The brick outfield wall at Wrigley is low and covered with Boston ivy and the outfield wall at Fenway is the Monster Wall, built high to shield games from folks drinking and eating at bars and restaurants across the street and watching without paying. Both share hand-placed score cards on the score board, but perhaps the most memorable sharing is that of Babe Ruth who played for the Red Sox and the Yankees. Babe Ruth was sold to the Yankees for $125,000. Ruth's fame and Boston's shame for trading him to the Yankees continues to this day. The Cubs dearly remember game 3 of the 1932 World Series when Babe allegedly pointed to a bleacher location and hit the next pitch there for a homer. We know the hit was true but the assigned location... Was it fact? Is it legend?

Now, both team ball parks will be on the way to fields of dreams legends for children in Waterville, Maine, 1160 miles east of Wrigley Field and 186 miles north of Fenway Park. Wrigley Field will join the two-thirds replica of Fenway Park in place for several years at a children's summer camp, a short distance from Waterville but Wrigley Field, to be known as Purnell Wrigley Field, will be in Waterville. Most impressive, however, is that they will be the ONLY two licensed replicated stadiums in the country where their spirit will be alive with children playing baseball with the hopes of perhaps one day becoming a legend.

As we look to the future, it is important to examine the past of the Chicago Cubs of Wrigley Field and the Boston Red Sox of Fenway Park, their players, their supporters, their fans, all of which make up the culture of baseball. It is also important to examine the dreamers, the players, the coaches, the supporters who made Purnell Wrigley Field happen in Waterville, and the dreams, dreamers, supporters, and local people with unique baseball connections who helped make the Maine's Fenway at Camp Tracy in Oakland, Maine, a reality.

CHICAGO:

Take me out to the ball game. Take me out with the crowd.
Buy me some peanuts and Cracker Jack. I don't care if I never get back.
Let me root, root, root for the home team. If they don't win it's a shame.
For it's one, two, three strikes you're out at the old ball game.
　　　　　　　　　　–Jack Norworth, 1908

BOSTON:

Hands, touchin' hands
Reachin' out touchin' me touchin' you.
Sweet Caroline
Good times never seemed so good.
I've been inclined
To believe they never would.
Warm, touchin' warm
Reachin' out. Touchin' me touchin' you.
Sweet Caroline...
　　　　　　　　–Neil Diamond, 1969

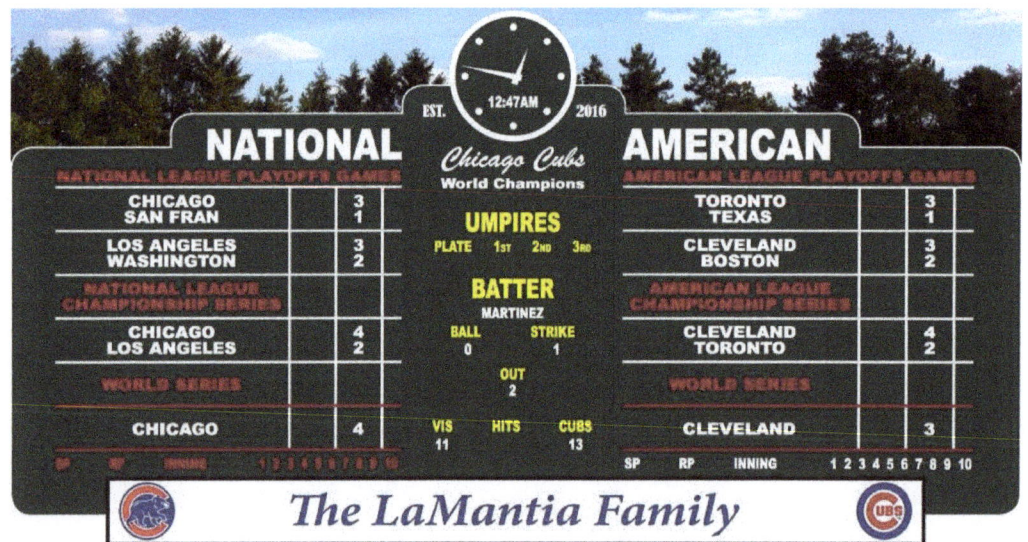

Purnell Wrigley scoreboard frozen in time at 12:47 a.m.
in honor of the Chicago Cubs winning their first World Series in 108 years.

IN THE BEGINNING

One day in the mid-60s, exact date unknown, Richard Hawkes, a Waterville banker, and Lester Jolovitz, a Waterville attorney, were invited by George Keller, Director of the Waterville YMCA, to look over land on McGrath (known locally as "McGraw") Pond Road in Oakland, a short drive from Waterville, as a possible site for a YMCA summer retreat for children. They found the 64 acres owned by Mrs. Mona A. Tracy suitable and plans were made to purchase the land. Honoring Mrs. Tracy's stipulation that the land retain the Tracy name, the deed signed on March 22, 1968 read in part that the Waterville Area Young Men's Christian Association now owned the Tracy land. Buildings for recreation, changing rooms, and daily activities were put up and that summer Camp Tracy became a reality, a summer day camp with eight week-long programs.

Richard Hawkes

Lester Jolovitz

George Keller

Ken Walsh came to the Waterville Boys and Girls Club in 1992 as its director and shortly thereafter was to meet philanthropist Harold Alfond at his home. It was a Monday night in 1993 and Mr. Alfond and his long-time friend John "Swisher" Mitchell, a player on the 1944 New England Championship Waterville basketball team and Senator George Mitchell's brother, were watching the Patriots play and Drew Bledsoe was on his way to scoring a touchdown. That done, Harold turned his attention to Ken: "What do you want?" Before Ken could answer, Mr. Alfond offered $50,000 for the next five years as a gift or a one-to-one challenge up to $500,000 to be raised in one year. John Mitchell encouraged Ken to choose the one-year challenge. Ken chose the one-to-one challenge and raised $2.1 million in the community to renovate the Boys and Girls Club.

IN THE BEGINNING

Realizing that three entities, including the Parks and Recreation Department, were vying for the same funds, Ken and the community leaders again approached Mr. Alfond and thus began the foundation of what was to become the Alfond Youth Center. Mr. Alfond's stipulations were met and in May, 1999, Senator George Mitchell, a Waterville native who with his brothers had spent many years at the Boys Club, along with General Colin Powell dedicated the Alfond Youth Center, the only facility in the country with the YMCA and the Boys and Girls Club combined in one facility.

It was time to look into developing Camp Tracy. The New Balance Foundation began a $1 million matching fund campaign. With the challenge met and other donations given, a lodge, cabins, outdoor theater, climbing walls, tennis courts, and rope courses were built. Camp Tracy was growing. However, something was missing.

Baseball had been a strong influence in Ken's youth and he realized a place for kids to play baseball at Camp Tracy was what was missing. Knowing Mr. Alfond was also a baseball fanatic, a Red Sox fan in particular, Ken shared his dream to build a baseball diamond in the two-tiered ball field at Camp Tracy. Mr. Alfond offered to help with the project by donating the first $50,000. Ken refused his offer and as a way of thanking him for all his years of support, said, "It will be our pleasure to give something to you." Thus, the idea to build a licensed replica of Fenway Park began as a gift and surprise to Harold Alfond.

Obtaining the licensing agreements from Major League Baseball and the Boston Red Sox was difficult. John Brody, Director of Marketing for Major League Baseball and a Waterville Boys and Girls Club alumnus, helped secure the licensing agreement with Major League Baseball and the Red Sox came through with a license to use the name Fenway Park. After six months of selling the project, the objective was accomplished. Contributions and sponsorships from various organizations, including the Red Sox Foundation and the Cal Ripken Sr. Foundation, began to flow in.

In the background are Bill Alfond, Ken Walsh, John Winkin and Governor John Baldacci.
Cal is presenting a signed framed jersey to Harold that is hung at the Alfond Youth Center library.

IN THE BEGINNING

On September 9, 2007, the two-thirds replica of Fenway Park was dedicated as the Harold Alfond Fenway Park. In attendance with Mr. Alfond and Ken were Cal Ripken Jr, the Governor, Congressmen, local dignitaries, guests, and the Boston Park Mounted unit. It was a rainy but glorious day for all those sharing the magic of the dedication of the Harold Alfond Fenway Park. There was now a Green Monster at Camp Tracy on "McGraw" Pond Road in Oakland, Maine.

After several years of successful programming at Maine's Fenway, another campaign was started to raise $500,000 to turf the field which would allow more play time for the children and less concern for northeast weather. Within a year money was raised and on June 21, 2014, Maine's Fenway Turf Dedication Ceremony took place. Jim Rice, Hall of Fame Red Sox outfielder, came for the dedication and threw out the first pitch. Another magical day at Harold Alfond Fenway Park in Oakland, Maine.

BASEBALL 1914-1918

Major League baseball during World War I was not seriously impacted despite its two hundred and fifty players in the military, others in the reserves, and others doing war-related work or playing ball in an industrial league. The few who were sent to Europe included Christy Mathewson, Ty Cobb, Pete Alexander, George Sister and Branch Rickey. On July 19, 1918, Secretary of War Newton Baker decided that baseball was not an essential occupation. Panic arose within the establishment but the season stayed open until Labor Day and it was "Play Ball" for the infamous 1918 World Series.

There were losses. Former White Sox farmhand John Cooper was killed in action in September 2, 1918. He was 30 years old. Eddie Grant, third baseman and leadoff hitter for the Phillies was 35 when he was killed on October 5, 1918, on a mission to rescue the fabled "Lost Battalion." Robert Troy, one-game Major Leaguer, was killed in action in France on October 7, 1918. And, on this side of the Atlantic, Spanish flu was detected at an army barracks in Kansas in March 1918 and quickly spread killing 675,000 worldwide within months. Uniformed baseball players who died from the flu included Harry Action, Larry Chappell, Harry Glen, John Inglis, Arthur Kimbro, Ralph Worrell. Uniformed Western Association umpire Frank Healey lost his life as well.

The National baseball Hall of Fame boasts that 64 of its members served in the Armed Forces during wartime. There are two baseball legends who served in World War I:

• Grover Alexander, known as "Old Pete," was a pitcher who played for the Philadelphia Phillies, Chicago Cubs, and St. Louis Cardinals. He served in France as Sergeant in the 432nd Field Artillery. His career included 90 shutouts (a national league record) and 373 wins.

• Eddie Collins was a second baseman who played for the Philadelphia Athletics and the Chicago White Sox. His resumé shows that he was the 6th player to have 3000 hits, that he was the only American League Player to steal bases six times in one game, and only one of four players with more than 500 steals and a .400 on-base percentage. His post-playing career found him as General Manager, Vice President, and part owner of the Boston Red Sox. Collins was brought up in Millerton, New York, where Ken Walsh played baseball in the field honoring his name – The Eddie Collins Field.

We are reminded on November 11 when we see red poppies for sale everywhere that those red poppies are the familiar emblem of Remembrance Day because of the poem "In Flanders Fields." Poppies bloomed across the worse battlefields of Flanders in World War I and the red of the poppy became the symbol for the blood spilled. Remember: on November 11 at the 11th hour of the 11th day of the 11th month of the year 1918, hostilities formally ended the Great War.

IN FLANDERS FIELDS
by John McCrae

In Flanders fields the poppies blow
Between the crosses, row on row.
That mark our place; and in the sky
The larks, still bravely singing, fly
Scarce heard amid the guns below.

We are the dead. Short days ago
We lived, felt dawn, saw sunset glow,
Loved and were loved, and now we lie
In Flanders fields.

Take up our quarrel with the foe:
To you from failing hands we throw
The torch; be yours to hold it high.
If ye break faith with us who die
We shall not sleep, though poppies grow
In Flanders fields.

BASEBALL 1914-1918

Millerton, New York, native HOF Eddie Collins

Grover Cleveland Alexander
American Major League Baseball pitcher

SUNDAY, DECEMBER 7, 1941

Sunday, December 7, 1941, a day forever etched in the souls of those alive and told and retold by them to those who were not. At 7:53 a.m., the Japanese attacked the United States Naval base at Pearl Harbor, Hawaii, resulting in five battleships sunk, eight damaged; three light cruisers, three destroyers and three smaller vessels lost along with 199 aircraft. Lives lost: 2,335 servicemen and 68 civilians; 1,178 wounded. To this day, it is said that the oil which continues to seep from the sunken USS Arizona is the tears of the over one thousand servicemen entombed in their watery grave.

Monday, December 8, 1941, President Roosevelt responded to both sessions of Congress. In part:

"Yesterday, December 7th, 1941, a date which will live in infamy, the United States of America was suddenly and deliberately attacked by naval and air forces of the Empire of Japan.

"It will be recorded that the distance of Hawaii from Japan makes it obvious that the attack was deliberately planned many days or even weeks ago. During the intervening time the Japanese government has deliberately sought to deceive the United States by false statements and expressions of hope for continued peace.

"Hostilities exist. There is no blinking at the fact that our people, our territory, and our interests are in grave danger.

"With the confidence in our armed forces with the unbounding determination of our people, we will gain the inevitable triumph. So help us God.

"I ask that the Congress declare that since the unprovoked and dastardly attack by Japan on Sunday, December 7th, 1941, a state of war has existed between the United States and the Japanese Empire." —President Franklin D. Roosevelt – December 8, 1941

SUNDAY, DECEMBER 7, 1941

America was at war with Japan.

Prior to that date, in 1940, a draft was put in place that for all men between 18 and 45, there would be a selection for one year's service in the National Lottery. 50,000,000 registered; 10,110,104 were drafted; and ultimately 8,700,000 men and women enlisted to serve in the army during World War II.

Spying was a given factor in both World War I and World War II and codes were developed to attempt to keep each from knowing what the other was doing. During World War I, the Germans learned of Allied tactical plans by tapping into their telephone lines and easily breaking their codes until a U.S. commander came up with the idea of using the Native American language Choctaw for the code. It paved the way for the Navajo Code Talkers in World War II.

Choctaw Code Talkers

The Choctaw Native Americans were farmers of corn, beans, and pumpkins and hunters, fishermen, and gatherers, as well as allies of the United States in the War of 1812. However, they and the Chickasaw, Creek, Seminole, Cherokee, the so-called "Five Civilized Tribes" which included Native Americans, African freedmen and slaves living among them, were forced by the Indian Removal Act of 1830 to cede millions of acres of their land to the government. Between 1830 and 1850, those tribes were forcibly relocated to an area west of the Mississippi River Valley, a journey by foot with thousands suffering from exposure, disease, and starvation. More than 4000 died before reaching their destinations. A "Trail of Tears" was how a Choctaw chief described the tragedy. The Choctaw found themselves in what is now Oklahoma.

When the United States entered the war in April, 1917, Native Americans were not citizens but that did not stop several thousand from enlisting: nearly 1,000 from 26 tribes in Texas and Oklahoma enlisted in the 36th division. They arrived in France in 1918 to participate in the Meuse-

SUNDAY, DECEMBER 7, 1941

Argonne campaign, a major offensive along the Western Front. Germans knew the plans as they were able to listen in on Allied communications and break their codes. As previously reported, the company commander in the 36th Division overheard two of his soldiers talking in Choctaw and recognized the potential use of the language as code. Thus, on October 26, 1918, the first five of an eventual nineteen Choctaw used their language to assist in the withdrawal of two companies from the front. Success. "Big gun," artillery; "little gun shoot fast", machine gun; "stone," grenade; "scalps," casualties. Code Talkers were born.

Trail of Tears Monument

TWO OUT OF TWENTY-NINE

Carl Nelson Gorman died February 1, 1998. Born on October 3, 1907, on the Navajo Reservation in Chinle, Arizona, to Navajo parents who were founders of the Presbyterian Mission on the reservation. Learning that the Marines were recruiting Navajos fluent in English and Navajo, he, at 34, was too old to enlist so lied about his age and became an Akalh B-kosi-lai: a United States Marine. Mr. Gorman was the oldest of the 29 Code Talkers.

The curse of the Navajo children became a blessing for some. Children were taken from families and sent to mission schools to be educated and clothed. Gone was their tribal language and dress. They would be taught English and speak English only; they would wear uniforms and wear uniforms only. Mr. Gorman, one of the removed Navajo children, recalled at mission school he "once had been chained to an iron pipe for a week because he insisted on speaking his native tongue." (*NY Times* 2/1/98)

Carl Gorman

Philip Johnston, son of Presbyterian missionaries on the Navajo reservation where Carl grew up, learned the Navajo language. In later years, Mr. Johnson, a civil engineer in Los Angeles, had read of the Army using Choctaw in military communications in World War I. Remembering his childhood and having learned the difficult Navajo language, he proposed to the Marines that they recruit Navajos who could speak English to develop a code which he felt the Japanese could not crack and might be a help in the battle for Iwo Jima.

The Navajo, like the Choctaw, had to develop a code for military usage. Ergo, the Navajo Code Talkers, now numbering 29 and ultimately 400, used bird names for various planes: tas-chizzie, or swallow for torpedo plane; jay-sho, or buzzard for bomber; da-he-tih-hi or humming bird for a fighter plane. It was felt that the Battle for Iwo Jima could not have been won without them. The most notable instance was the following sequence: Mount dibeh (Sheep), no-dah-ih (Ute), gah (Rabbit), tkin (Ice) shush (Bear), wol-la-chee (Ant), moasi (Cat), lin (Horse), yeh-hes (Itch): spelling S-U-R-I-B-A-C-H-I. The Navajo code notified the Pacific command that the Marines had planted the American flag on Mount Suribachi on Iwo Jima. Included in the iconic photograph of the flag being raised on Iwo Jima is Native American Ira Hamilton Hayes of the Pima tribe of Arizona. Mr. Hayes is the first marine on the left in that photograph.

After the war, Mr. Gorman became a prominent artist who taught at the University of California but ultimately settled in Fort Defiance, Arizona, where he continued to paint. His artistic legacy was passed on to his son R. C. Gorman, a prominent master of oil paints, lithography and sculpture who lived in Taos, New Mexico.

Chester Nez, the last living Code Talker, was born January 23, 1921, into the Chi Chil Tah, Jones Ranch, New Mexico. His actual first and surname are lost to history. Eight years old at missionary school, he was given the name "Chester" after Chester "I may be President of the United States but my private life is nobody's damned business" Arthur, 21st President. He, like Carl Gorman, was taught to speak English and was to speak English only.

Before the schooling, he herded sheep and goats, slept under the stars, ran miles, liked danger. He was a Navajo warrior and protector. Attending the Tuba City Boarding School, the Marines came in 1942 looking for young Navajo boys who spoke their native language and understood English. Chester Nez could defend his country and make his family proud. He signed up as he was ready for an adventure that would allow him to see what was on the other side of the buttes. Becoming a member of the all-Navajo 382nd Marine Platoon suited him well. He would become one of the original 29 Code Talkers and become part of those on Iwo Jima who were helpful in taking the island from Japan. Navajo religion forbids contact with the dead and being spooked by the battlefield stench of the dead, he would say a Navajo prayer and touch the buckskin medicine bag filled with blessed corn pollen and tiny secret souvenirs which he wore around his neck.

TWO OUT OF TWENTY-NINE

Chester Nez, now 83, on April 10, 2004, with that same buckskin medicine bag in his left hand and a baseball in his right and saying a Navajo prayer for the Red Sox, threw that baseball for a strike down the middle as the ceremonial first pitch for the Red Sox second home game. Before the pitch, Mr. Nez "did a blessing for all the spectators who were there. And, then I said a blessing for the Red Sox to do well and keep winning their games from then on." (AP, 2004) After the pitch, Mr. Nez stayed on the mound, faced east, took out some corn powder and began a blessing for the Red Sox Nation. The Sox won seven out of nine games.

Living in Albuquerque and learning the Red Sox had fallen behind 3-0 to the Yankees in the American League Championship Series, Mr. Nez stepped outside his home, faced east, and said another Navajo blessing. The Red Sox had four straight wins over the Yankees, the first time in Major League Baseball history that a team came back to win a seven-game series after being down 3-0. "I think that they just might come through." The curse of the Babe broken by a Navajo prayer and the corn contents in a Navajo's buckskin medicine bag?

Chester Nez

Chester Nez

Chester Nez, the last of the original 29 Code Talkers, died June 4, 2014. Marine veteran Michael Smith whose late father was a Code Talker wept as he described Mr. Nez as a "quiet, humble" Navajo Marine. The all-Navajo 382nd Marine Platoon is "the chapter about the first Navajo Code Talkers coming to a close. People talk about it, and you never think it's going to happen in your lifetime. They are carrying the past with them. To see this in a lifetime, it's sad. I hope it makes us (Navajo) people stronger." Other Navajo veterans mourners echoed Mr. Smith's sentiment saying Nez "baa hane' yée éi t'aa kodiiji' biighah silii." His life story ends here. (courtesy freerepublic.com)

The Choctaw and Navajo codes were never cracked.

April 14, 1921 - February 18, 2017. Retired Marine Lt. General Lawrence Snowden, age 95 and thought to be the oldest survivor of the battle for Iwo Jima, has died, a day before the 72nd anniversary of the beginning of the battle. He was a 23-year-old captain when he led a company of 230 Marines ashore at Iwo Jima; more than half of them were killed in the battle. He was wounded but persuaded commanders to let him return to fighting after his first evacuation. His career found him not only serving in World War II but in the Korean War and in Vietnam. During his career, General Snowden rose to three-star rank and was assistant commandant of the Marine Corp before his retirement in 1979.

After the Korean War, he was assigned to a logistics conference in Japan and as he got to know some of that nation's military officers, business, and government leaders, he decided they were not to blame for the war, but were honorably doing their duty at Iwo Jima. He participated in the 1985 "Reunion of Honor" mission which met on Iwo Jima with Japanese veterans of the battle and in 1995, he was instrumental in setting up another reunion to mark the 50th Anniversary of the battle.

The chapter "The Declining Decade" from his memoir *Snowden's Story*, published in 2016, recounts the infirmities of old age, the inevitability of change: "From a statistical standpoint, it can be expected that God will probably call me home to the big Marine Corps base in the sky sometime in the 2016-20 time frame and I think I will be ready for that." (*Naples Daily News*)

Godspeed, General Snowden.

General Lawrence Snowden

THURSDAY, DECEMBER 11, 1941

December 11, 1941. Germany declares war on the United States.
December 11, 1941. Congress declares war on Germany.
January 3, 1942. A declaration by Congress read, in part:

"JOINT RESOLUTION Declaring That a State of War Exists Between The Government of Germany and the Government and the People of the United States and Making Provisions To Prosecute The Same.

…That the state of war between the United States and the Government of Germany which has thus been thrust upon the United States is hereby formally declared; and the President is hereby authorized and directed to employ the entire naval and military forces of the United States… to bring the conflict to a successful termination, all of the resources of the country are hereby pledged by the Congress of the United States."

(Signed) Sam Rayburn, Speaker of the House of Representatives
(Signed) H. A. Wallace, Vice President of the United States and President of the Senate
Approved December 11, 1941 3:05 PM E.S.T.
(Signed) Franklin D. Roosevelt.

America was unprepared for war with Japan, let alone with Germany. A massive effort to enlist the services of the country was afoot. Millions of women worked the jobs of the men who were now in the armed services. "Rosie the Riveter" became the icon of those women. Men who could not serve helped out policing the country. (On a personal note. My mother worked at a "filter center" somewhere in downtown Portland. We were never told where and only that they spotted planes. My father became a nighttime policeman as there were blackouts and no traffic lights. He would leave the house with a flashlight and a "billy club" and direct traffic. Mrs. Strout on our street had three blue stars hanging in a window for those serving and a gold for one killed. BRJ).

THURSDAY, DECEMBER 11, 1941

THE LONELY HILL by RA Harris

Wild grow the poppies in Tunisian vale
Gracing the green of a fertile land
And here comes "Peace" to lay her veil
On the hill of the foes last stand.

Out of the Plain reared the lonely hill
Like a breast bared to the sky
Its slopes clasped the fallen ever still
And its bosom echoed the swallow's cry.

Small sanctuary of a fallen dream
Last bastion to Enfidaville
Your crumbled fort is a desolate scene
Where all but the winds are still.

The winds will rise and the tall grass bend
To ripple like waves of the sea
And time will take the scars to mend
On the lonely hill of the free.

U-BOATS FAR AND NEAR

Germany had Unterseeboots – U-boots or U-boats as referred to by Americans. They were used in World War I after Germany announced on January 30, 1917, that its U-boots would engage in unrestricted warfare beginning February 1st. On March 17, 1917, submarines sank three American vessels. The United States declared war on Germany on April 12, 1917.

During World War II, U-boats attacked vessels while on the surface and they could travel about 60 miles underwater before having to surface for fresh air. Under water, they fired torpedoes up to twenty-two feet long which could travel thirty miles per hour. They found their way to American waters and to attacking ships off the North Carolina Outer Banks. Those shipping lanes became known as "Torpedo junction." Reports of enemies attacking ships were kept confidential but those living in the area knew exactly what was happening. And these boats had ways of getting spies on American soil.

June 4, 1944. The USS *Guadalcanal* of the United States Navy Task Group 22.3 belonged to a hunter-killer group of battleships looking for German submarines. She found one and captured *U-505* off Cape Blanco in French West Africa. All but one member of its crew survived the capture. The *U-505* was towed to Bermuda as top secret because of the information retrieved from *U-505*; from there, it was towed to Ruston, Louisiana, by the tug boat Abnaki. (Abnaki is the name of a group of Native Americans in the Eastern part of the United States and Canada with similar culture and language; five Maine Native American tribes are included in the Abnaki.) Interned at Camp Ruston, the captured crew, still considered top secret, was not even allowed visits by the International Red Cross. Ultimately, the crew was declared dead by the German government. After the war, they were sent to Great Britain for two years and released in 1947.

U-505

Among the guards were members of the U. S. Navy baseball team, composed mostly of minor league professional players who had previously toured combat areas entertaining the troops. The guards started teaching some of the *U-505* sailors to play baseball. Among the teachers was Gene Moore who was signed by the Brooklyn Dodgers in 1940 at age 15, and it was the Dodgers who arranged for him to join the traveling Navy baseball team. It was there that Moore broke an ankle in a game which limited his future baseball days. Shortly before his death in 1983 at 57 years, he told his son Gary his story which Gary documented in his book, *Playing with the Enemy*. It was made into a movie of the same name with Gene Moore's grandson Toby Moore playing the role of his grandfather.

The capture of the *U-505* was the first ship captured on the high seas since the War of 1812 when the *Constitution* was victorious over the *Guerriere*.

Fish Out of Water by Wesley Harris documents the lives of other prisoners at Camp Ruston, including prisoners from *U-234* which was engaged in a mission to take military technology and uranium for atomic bombs to Japan when Japan surrendered.

PROTECTING MAINE'S COAST

Harvard Hodgkins, an Eagle Scout and a high school senior in Hancock Point, Maine, near Bar Harbor, was returning from a school dance on November 29, 1944, when he came upon two men walking, wearing topcoats and carrying briefcases. He reckoned that two men walking in 20-degree weather dressed as they were in hunting season could not be Mainers. E. B. White quipped in *One Man's Meat* that no one in his right mind in Maine at the end of November would wear anything other than a jacket to keep in the body's warmth. Only spies would dress in topcoats.

Young Mr. Hodgkins went home and told his sheriff father who notified the FBI. At daylight, a rubber raft was found hidden in the rocks at the beach where they had been dropped off. It was later learned that the spies continued walking along a road and were passed by two cars. The drivers thought it strange seeing two men walking at that late hour. Neither stopped. Folks from Hancock minded their own business. Upon reaching Route 1, a third car passed them and stopped. It was a taxi who gave them a ride to the Bangor train station, 35 miles away – the fare was $6.00 – and they made their way to Portland and ultimately to New York. Erich Gimpel, a German who was schooled in spying, and William Colepaugh, a pro-German American, were eventually found, tried as spies, and sentenced to death by hanging. Before their sentences were carried out, President Roosevelt died and all federal executions were suspended for four weeks. By that time, the war had ended in Europe and President Harry S. Truman commuted the two sentences to life in prison – Gimbel's because the U.S. and Germany were no longer at war and Colepaugh because he had given himself up and provided the FBI with information needed to arrest Gimpel. Colepaugh served 17 years in prison and died in Florida in March 2005. Gimpel served ten years at Leavenworth, Alcatraz and Atlanta. Released in 1954 and deported to Germany, he later moved to Brazil and died there September 2010, in his 94th year.

Captured spies - AP photo

Harvard Hodgkins? He was the talk of the country. The *New York Journal-American* sponsored his first ride in a plane, bringing him and his family to New York for a week in January 1946. He was given the key to the city. He saw the Statue of Liberty, went to Radio City Music Hall, some Broadway shows and met Joe Louis and Babe Ruth. He received a full scholarship to the Maine Maritime Academy. He died in May 1984.

In addition to the Hancock spies and North Carolina's U-boat problems, Portland Harbor in the Gulf of Maine was long before recognized as being in need of navigational assistance. Ergo, in 1787, when Maine was still part of Massachusetts, George Washington directed that a lighthouse be built on Portland Head; thus, Portland Head Light. At a cost of $1500, the oldest lighthouse in Maine was operational on January 10, 1791. Whale oil lamps were the source of light until 1855 when Fresnel lenses, slender lenses with specific aperture and focal lengths as used in camera lenses, were installed giving light 20 miles out to sea.

Fresnel lens

Portland Head Light

Casco Bay is rife with the remains of old forts built to defend Portland Harbor. One seen by all who come to Portland by sea is Fort Gorges on Hog Island Ledge built in the middle of the harbor during the Civil War. Batteries continued to be installed throughout the years and by 1942, military reservations were installed on Cape Elizabeth (Fort Williams), Peaks Island, Jewel Island, Long Island, Bailey Island, and Chebeague.

Fort Williams, built on 14 acres near Portland Head Light, became fortified with three batteries in 1885, shortly before the Spanish-American War and continued to be fortified throughout the various wars. Between 1900 and 1911, the Fort, now on 90.45 acres, continued to grow. Included in the growth were enlisted barracks, non-commissioned and commissioned officers' quarters, hospital, gymnasium, post exchange, bakery, abattoir, commissary, laundry, et cetera. It was a facility totally able to handle the lives of those stationed there. It also included a baseball diamond with concrete bleachers for recreational needs.

Fort Williams served as headquarters of the Harbor Defenses of Portland throughout World War II. It is now owned and run by the Town of Cape Elizabeth. The Army post was decommissioned in 1963 and buildings are largely demolished. It is a family place now to picnic, run, play tennis on its two courts, and play baseball on its baseball diamond – all within view of Portland Head Light.

BASEBALL 1942-1945

PLAY BALL: BASEBALL IN THE WAR

Birdie Tebbetts was on the Island of Guam during the battle for Iwo Jima. As captain in charge of morale for the Army Air Force, he made sure baseball played a big part in his daily activities and assembled a team of players that included former big leaguers Max West (Braves), Joe Gordon (Yankees), Howie Pollett (Cardinals) and Tex Hughson (Red Sox). Fighting on Iwo Jima was coming to an end so Tebbetts' team was dispatched there to play for the troops. Quoting Tebbetts from his autobiography *Birdie: Confessions of a Baseball Nomad*, he recalled, "Our B-24s circled the pockmarked airstrip (on Iwo Jima), and put down for a bumpy landing. It was plain to see that just the day before our guys had been in the midst of a fierce battle; smoke was still rising from burnt-out emplacements and caves."

Birdie Tebbetts

The "Seabees", the Navy's construction crew, bulldozed a diamond out of a rock; its outfield boundaries being the Pacific Ocean. Chalk lines were laid out and empty bomb crates and packing cases were used as bleachers. "When we got suited up and went out there to warm up, I look around and there were GIs and Marines standing on top of boxes, hanging off cranes, trucks and jeeps...our job...was simple. To put on a big-league ballgame for 12,000 grimy, cheering, gun-toting, battle-torn soldiers and marines. To take their minds off the sheer horror of what they had just been through. They came on foot, by jeep, truck, a tank or two, and even some on crutches. It was an incredible sight."

The game was a huge morale booster. Tebbetts was approached by a Marine colonel who told him the ballgame was a lifesaver. Walking away, he turned to Tebbetts and said, "This is the most important game you'll ever play, Captain Tebbetts."

In 1944, the Seabees built another baseball field in the side of a hill on Iwo Jima, built stands, and named it Higashi (Japanese for east) Field. Tebbetts returned with three teams: the 58th Bombardment Wing Wingmen, the 73rd Bombardment Wing Bombers and the 313th Bombardment Wing Flyers. Forty-eight players were divided between three teams: the Wingmen were led by Tebbetts and included Enos Slaughter, Joe Gordon, Joe Marty, Billy Hitchcock, Howie Pollet and Chubby Dean; The 73rd Bombardment Wing Bombers, managed by Buster Mills, included Stan Rojek, Taft Wright, Mike McCormick, Tex Hughson and Sid Hudson; the 313th Bombardment Wing Flyers was managed by Lew Riggs and his team included Johnny Sturm, Max West, Walt Judnich, and Stan Goletz.

The ballgames proved so popular, recalled Rugger Ardizoia of the 113th Flyers who was a Yankees farmhand before military service, that "playing for the troops we had over 10,000 watching us while a big named band had only about 1,000. The band leader was so disgusted he decided to pack up and leave while we carried on playing." With the exception of a few, the return to baseball by many players who played on Iwo Jima was not successful. However, their baseball successes there on that remote island in the Pacific were unrivaled.

1942-1945: BASEBALL AT HOME

The country was fighting the war at home by manufacturing ammunition, guns, and other war necessities. With the men at war, women were working full time building ships and planes. Hillerich & Bradsby, makers of the famous Louisville Slugger baseball bats, turned their wood-turning equipment into the production of stocks for the M1 carbine rifle. America had become the "Arsenal of Democracy."

It was questionable if baseball would survive the war. It remembered World War I had ended the 1918 season on September 2, and the armistice agreement saved the following season. After the attack on Pearl Harbor, President Roosevelt stepped up to the plate and said, "I honestly feel that it would be best for the country to keep baseball going" and went so far as to add that he would like to see more night games that hard-working people could attend. He felt baseball could provide entertainment for at least 20 million people. Although the quality of the teams might be lowered by the greater use of older players replacing young men going into military service, the popularity of the sport would continue.

Players enlisted or were drafted from the beginning of the war, but there was an undertone of displeasure towards seemingly fit men still playing and evading military service. Understandable, but ultimately there was no question that baseball was a morale booster. Private John E. Stevenson, based at Fort Dix, New Jersey, wrote, "Baseball is part of the American way of life. Remove it and you remove something from the lives of American citizens, soldiers and sailors." Private Clifford P. Mansfield of Fort Knox, Kentucky, echoed the thought, "For the morale of the soldiers and the morale of America itself, 'keep 'em playing'."

With the majority of known players serving their country, room was made for others to play. That included Pete Gray, née Peter Wyshner, taking the name Gray from his brother Whitey Gray, a professional boxer. Pete Gray went on to play for the Major League Baseball St. Louis Browns in 1945 where he played 77 games, completing 51 hits, batting a .218. He was released the following year.

Pete Gray was right-handed until he lost his right arm at age seven in a truck accident in 1923. The arm had to be amputated above the elbow. He loved baseball and taught himself to bat and field one-handed, catching the ball in his glove and then quickly removing his glove and transferring the ball to his hand in one motion. Completing his formal education at age 13, he began working as a water boy at the Truesdale (Pennsylvania) Colliery. He would not accept sympathy nor being treated differently from others. While playing sand lot baseball, the story goes that he ran home and crashed into the catcher and knocked the ball out of the catcher's glove. Safe! The upset catcher said he would have hit him if he had had two arms. Pete got in his face and said, "Go ahead and try."

Pete Gray played professional baseball with one arm.
He was an inspiration to the nation.

At 19, he was playing for several minor leagues. He had tryouts with the St. Louis Browns and Philadelphia Athletics but was never called up by either team. In 1941, after the attack on Pearl Harbor, he attempted to join the army and was denied on the basis that he was an amputee. "If I could teach myself how to play baseball with one arm, I sure as hell could handle a rifle." His speed and place hitting made him a successful outfielder in the minor leagues. His batting average of .333 and a stolen base record of 68 got him named the 1944 Southern Association's Most Valuable Player and was recognized by the Philadelphia Sports Writers Association as the "Most Courageous Athlete." Pete responded: "Boys, I can't fight and so there is no courage about me. Courage belongs on the battlefield, not on the baseball diamond." Twelve minor leagues survived during the war years compared to 44 circuits that operated in 1940. Pete Gray went on to play for the Major League Baseball St. Louis Browns in 1945 where he played 77 games, completing 51 hits and batting a .218. He was released the following year.

1945. The war was won, troops returned and those who did not were mourned. Ted Williams, Joe DiMaggio, "Yogi" Berra, Jackie Robinson and other baseball players traded in their military uniforms for baseball uniforms. Fans were eating peanuts and Cracker Jack; they were eating hot dogs; they were drinking beer; they were cheering their favorite team and booing the visiting team. They were back where they left off – baseball as they knew it was back. It was PLAY BALL: "one, two, three strikes and you're out..."

THE FINAL WORD: WE HAVE NOT FORGOTTEN

16,500,000 men and women served in the military in World War II, 70,000 on Iwo Jima alone. 48,231,700 people worldwide lost their lives as a result of World War II, 7,000 on Iwo Jima alone. Countless others served behind the lines. One among many was Hungarian-born Hannah Senesh who left Hungary when she was 18 for the British Mandate of Palestine, joined the British Army and became one of 37 parachutists of Mandate Palestine parachuted by the British Army into Yugoslavia. Their mission was to assist in the rescue of Hungarian Jews about to be deported to the German death camp at Auschwitz. Captured on the Hungarian border and tortured for five months, she was shot to death by a German firing squad on November 7, 1944. She was 23.

Hannah Senesh was a poet and we offer one of her poems in remembrance of those who died in war.

> "There are stars whose radiance is visible on Earth though they have long been extinct. There are people whose brilliance continues to light the world even though they are no longer among the living. These lights are particularly bright when the night is dark. They light the way for humankind."

Hannah Senesh

THE REMAINING FOUR

500 Baseball players served in World War II
64 National Baseball Hall of Fame Members served in World War II
4 Baseball legends served in World War II

1. Lawrence Peter "Yogi" Berra, May 12, 1928 - September 22, 2015. His nickname "Yogi," the only name he was known by, came from his friend Jack Maguire while playing American Legion baseball: "He resembled a Hindu yogi whenever he sat around with arms and legs crossed waiting to bat or while looking sad after losing a game."

His first few years playing professional baseball were sidelined to serve in the Navy during World War II. He was a gunner and participated in the D-Day invasion. He returned to baseball in 1946 and ultimately become a three-time American League MVP Award winner, a ten-time World Series champion, and a 15-time All Star.

Yogi Berra

Admittedly one of the greatest catchers in baseball, he was equally well known for his daft quips:

"Baseball is ninety percent mental. The other half is physical."
"It's like deja vu all over again."
"I never said most of the things I said."
"All pitchers are liars or crybabies."

THE REMAINING FOUR

Mel Ott: "He seemed to be doing everything wrong, yet everything came out right. He stopped everything behind the plate and hit everything in front of it."

Yogi Berra's #8 was retired by the New York Yankees on July 22, 1972, and he was inducted into the Baseball Hall of Fame in that same year.

Yogi died September 22, 2015.

2. Joe DiMaggio, November 25, 1914 - March 8, 1999. Known as "The Yankee Clipper," Joe was a New York Yankees center fielder who had a 56-game hitting streak in 1941 which began on May 15 and ended July 17. Being "invited" to enlist in the Army Air Force in 1943, he was stationed at the Santa Ana Air Base in California and spent most of his time in the military playing on baseball teams as a way to entertain the troops and boost morale. He never served in combat. He returned to a brilliant career with the New York Yankees. Perhaps as well known as his baseball career was his marriage to Marilyn Monroe.

Joe was inducted into the Baseball Hall of Fame in 1955.

Joe DiMaggio's #5 was retired by the New York Yankees on April 18, 1958.

Joe DiMaggio

3. Jackie Robinson, January 31, 1919 - October 24, 1972. Baseball's curse of color was broken April 15, 1947, when Jackie Robinson became the first African American to play major league baseball. He was second baseman for the Brooklyn Dodgers and eventually led the Dodgers to six pennants and one World Series.

In 1942, Robinson was drafted and assigned to a segregated Army cavalry unit in Fort Riley, Kansas. He and several other black soldiers applied for admission to Officer Candidate School at Ft. Riley. Their applications were delayed until protests by heavyweight champion Joe Louis, stationed at Ft. Riley, and Truman Gibson, an assistant civilian aide to the Secretary of War, got them accepted into the school. It resulted in a life-long friendship with Joe Louis.

Robinson was reassigned to Fort Hood, Texas, where he joined the 761st "Black Panthers" Tank Battalion. An event on July 6, 1944, derailed his military career. While waiting results of hospital tests on an ankle he injured in junior college, he boarded an Army bus, an Army unsegregated bus, and the driver ordered him to move to the back of the bus. Robinson refused. The driver backed down but at the end of the line, summoned the military police who took Robinson into custody. The investigating officer recommended a court-martial. However, his commander, Paul L. Bates, refused to authorize the legal action. Transferred to the 758th Battalion, his commander there charged him with multiple offenses, including public drunkenness though Robinson did not drink. Court-martialed, he was ultimately acquitted by an all-white panel. His court-martial proceedings prohibited him from being deployed. He never saw combat action. His former unit, the 761st Tank Battalion, became the first black tank unit to see combat in World War II. The segregation matter would be vividly remembered when he tried to get into Major League Baseball.

Jackie Robinson

After his acquittal, he was transferred to Camp Breckinridge, Kentucky, where he served as a coach for army athletics. He was discharged in November 1944. While there he met a former player for the Kansas City Monarchs of the Negro American League who encouraged him to write to the Monarchs and ask for a tryout. He was accepted and offered a contract for $400 per month to play for them. The Red Sox held a tryout at Fenway Park for Robinson and other black players on April 16, 1944. It was a farce, designed to assuage segregation feelings of a powerful Boston City Councilman Isadore Muchnick. The stands were limited to management who subjected Robinson to racial epithets. He was humiliated. It was more than 14 years later, in July 1959, that the Boston Red Sox became the last major league team to integrate their roster.

Other teams had serious interest in signing a black ballplayer. Branch Rickey, club president and general manager of the Brooklyn Dodgers, began scouting Negro leagues for a possible addition to the Dodgers' roster with the help of scout Clyde Sukeforth, a Maine native. He selected Robinson from a list of promising black players and interviewed him for a possible assignment to Brooklyn's International League farm club, the Montreal Royals. The three-hour interview elicited the following exchange regarding race: Robinson: "Are you looking for a Negro who is afraid to fight back?" Rickey replied that he needed a Negro player "with guts enough not to fight back." Robinson agreed to "turn the other cheek." Rickey signed him to a contract for $600 a month. On October 23, 1946, it was publicly announced that Robinson would be assigned to the Royals for the 1946 season. His signed contract became known as "The Noble Experiment." Jackie Robinson was the first black baseball player in the International League since the 1880s.

Spring training in Florida was fraught with racism. He was not allowed to stay with his teammates at the team hotel; several teams turned down any event involving Robinson or Johnny Wright, another black player whom Rickey had signed up; the police chief of Sanford threatened to cancel games if Robinson and Wright did not cease training activities there. Robinson was sent to Daytona Beach. On March 17, 1946, in an exhibition game against the team's parent club, the Dodgers, Robinson became the first black player to openly play for a Minor League team against a Major League team. In 1947, Jackie Robinson was called up to play for the Brooklyn Dodgers. He played for them for ten years. In 1947, he was Rookie of the Year; in 1949 he was Most Valuable Player; in 1955, he was a World Series champion.

Jackie was inducted into the Baseball Hall of Fame July 23, 1962.

Jackie Robinson's #42 was retired by the Brooklyn Dodgers on June 4, 1972.

4. Ted Williams, August 30, 1918 - July 5, 2003. "The Kid", "The Splendid Splinter", "Teddy Ballgame", "The Thumper", "The Greatest Hitter Who Ever Lived". Those nicknames belong to Ted Williams who spent his 19-year Major League Baseball career – 1939-1942 and 1946-1960 – as a left fielder for the Boston Red Sox.

The years between 1943 and 1946? Upon receiving notice he was going to be drafted to serve in World War II, he fought the draft board and got them to classify him as being unable to serve due to the fact that he was the sole supporter of his mother. The press found out and did not take kindly to it nor did the public, calling him "unpatriotic". Ergo, he signed up in 1942 and served in the U.S. Navy and U.S. Marine Corp, and was promoted to second lieutenant. He returned to baseball in 1946 and won his first American League Most Valuable Player and played in his only World Series. In 1947, he won his second Triple Crown. He was called from inactive reserves to active military duty for portions of the 1952-1953 series to serve as a Marine combat aviator in the Korean War. In 1957 and 1958, he was the American League batting champion for the fifth and sixth times.

Williams retired from the Boston Red Sox in 1960 and devoted time to another passion: fishing. He hosted a television program about fishing and was inducted into the International Game Fish Association (IGFA) Fishing Hall of Fame. He raised millions of dollars for the Jimmy Fund cancer care and research. In 1991, President George H. W. Bush presented him with the presidential Medal of Freedom, the highest civilian award bestowed by the United States government. He was selected for the Major League All-Time team in 1997 and the Major League Baseball All-Century Team in 1999. Ted often came to Maine to fish and visit with his friend Harold Alfond. Harold was the first Maine minority owner of the Red Sox. Ted also recruited Maine's baseball coach John Winkin to run his youth baseball camp.

Ted was inducted into the Baseball Hall of Fame January 20, 1966.

Ted Williams' #9 was retired by the Boston Red Sox on May 29, 1984.

Ted Williams

"LUCKY CHARLIE"

Charles H. "Lucky Charlie" Weeghman, March 12, 1874 - November 1, 1938, was one of the founders of the major league baseball organization in Chicago, originally called the Federal League. It lasted two years: 1914-1915. As a young man, Weeghman worked for $10 a week as a waiter for Charlie King who ran a successful restaurant catering to newspaper men. Weeghman eventually owned 15 lunch counters in the Chicago area, the first one opening on the day Charlie King died. "Lucky Charlie" made a quick fortune in lunch counters and was said to be worth an estimated $8,000,000.

In 1911, Charles Weeghman made an unsuccessful attempt to purchase controlling interest in the St. Louis Cardinals. He founded the Chicago Whales in 1914 and built a steel and concrete ballpark for them on land he leased from a Theological Seminary for 99 years at a cost of $16,000. After the Federal League closed in 1915, he merged his Whales with the Chicago Cubs and moved them from its wooden West Side Park to Weeghman Park, the park name changing through the years from Weeghman Park to Cubs Park in 1920 to Wrigley Field in 1926. Remaining part of the Weeghman legacy, in addition to his still-standing park, is Ladies Day every Friday and fans allowed to keep foul balls which previously had to be returned to the club.

Charles Weeghman

The Cubs played the Cincinnati Reds on their first game at Weeghman Park on April 20, 1916. It went 11 innings, the highlight of the season. The Cubs won the National league pennant in 1918 aided by the season ending on September 1 because of World War I. With the Cubs struggling for cash, Weeghman rented Comiskey park for the Cubs' home game against the Red Sox in the World Series. Attendance was not much better; further, the Red Sox had played in Comiskey Park, knew the park, and the Cubs lost the series to Babe Ruth and the Sox in six games.

Perhaps that loss was the final blow that pushed Weeghman out of management. A number of investors had taken minority shares in the club, including chewing gum magnate William Wrigley. With Weeghman's finances in continuing decline, in November 1918 he gave up his remaining interest to Wrigley, resigned as president, and left baseball for good. Wrigley acquired complete control of the Cubs by 1921. Weeghman also lost control of his restaurant business and his brother Albert took it over. He moved to New York where he was unsuccessful in starting over in the restaurant business. On August 16, 1921, "Lucky Charlie" sponsored the first statewide rally of the Ku Klux Klan on his property in Lake Zurich, Illinois. On November 1, 1938, at the Drake Hotel in Chicago, Charles H. "Lucky Charlie" Weeghman suffered a fatal stroke.

SPEARMINT AND JUICY FRUIT BUY THE CUBS

William Wrigley Jr., September 30, 1867 - January 26, 1932, as a young boy with a basket of soap over his arm was peddling his father's Scouring Soap through the streets of Philadelphia. As a teenager, he traded the basket for a horse and wagon and went from town to town as a traveling soap salesman. At age 29 in 1891, he struck out for Chicago and continued to be a Wrigley soap distributor of his father's Scouring Soap.

William Wrigley, Jr.

He started offering a baking powder premium with each box of soap and then began selling baking powder with two free packages of chewing gum as a premium. The chewing gum was so popular that he dropped the soap and baking powder and voilà, in 1892, William Wrigley Jr. was in the chewing gum business. In 1893, he introduced and advertised Spearmint chewing gum, introduced Juicy Fruit gum in 1893, and by 1908, sales of Spearmint were estimated to be more than $1,000,000. In 1911, William Wrigley took over Zeno Manufacturing, the company that made his chewing gum, and established the Wm. Wrigley Jr. Company. By 1925, Wrigley turned the company presidency over to his son Philip and became chairman of the board. By that time, the company had factories making chewing gum in the United States, Canada, and Australia.

By 1921, William Wrigley Jr. was a majority stockholder in The Chicago Cubs. After his death in 1932, his son Philip became a majority stockholder, followed by his son William assuming

control upon Philip's death in 1977. On June 16, 1981, it was announced that the Chicago Cubs had been sold to the Tribune Company, parent of the *Chicago Tribune* and *The Daily News* in New York. Eighty one percent of the ownership was transferred and all remaining 1900 shares in baseball's only publicly owned corporation. The sale included Wrigley Field and all the team debts. Thus ended the legacy of the oldest family tie to one team in major league baseball.

In January 2009 a Ricketts family bid led by Thomas S. Ricketts, born May 23, 1965, and son of J. Joseph Ricketts, founder of Ameritrade, was chosen as the winning bidder for the Chicago Cubs. The bid was estimated at $875 million for the team and related assets. On October 31, 2009, Thomas S. Ricketts was introduced as the chairman of the Chicago Cubs. He, his four siblings, and his parents share interest in the team through their family trust. Will this be a Ricketts legacy at Wrigley Field?

Thomas S. Ricketts

A CURSE BECOMES A LEGEND

The Curse of the Billy Goat

1945. Wrigley Field. Game four of the World Series between the Chicago Cubs and the Detroit Tigers. Fan Billy Sianis, owner of Billy Goat Tavern, has two tickets for the game – one for himself and one for his billy goat Murphy. When asked to leave the game because Murphy's odor was bothering other fans, Mr. Sianis was outraged and allegedly declared "Them Cubs, they ain't gonna win no more," "win no more" being interpreted by some to mean there would never be another World Series game won at Wrigley Field. They have not since 1908 nor played in one since 1945. The curse?

There are different interpretations as to just what Mr. Sianis's outburst meant. Would World Series games ever again be played at Wrigley Field? Would the Cubs ever appear in the World Series anyplace? Perhaps both. The Sianis family claims that Murphy's proud owner sent a telegram to Cubs' team owner Philip Wrigley: "You are going to lose this World Series and you are never going to win another World Series again. You are never going to win a World Series again because you insulted my goat." The language appears a little different but it matters not. A curse is a curse. The Cubs were up two games to one in the 1945 Series, ended up losing Game 4 as well as the best-of-seven series, four games to three. The curse?

Attempts to break the curse have included Billy Sianis's nephew Sam being brought to Wrigley Field many times with a goat in an attempt to break the curse: on Opening Day in 1984 and 1989 when the Cubs actually won their division; in 1994 to stop a home losing streak; and in 1998 for the Wild Card play-in game which they won. Further attempts have included a butchered head hung from the Harry Caray statue on October 3, 2007. Winning in 2007 and 2008 division titles, they were swept away by the Arizona Diamondbacks and the Los Angeles Dodgers, respectively. The elimination by Arizona came on October 6, the same date Billy Sianis and goat Murphy attended the game at Wrigley Field in 1945. The curse?

Intervening years in attempts to get rid of the curse have included a Greek Orthodox priest spraying holy water in and around the Cubs' dugout in 2008 to a group of five Chicago Cubs fans calling themselves "Crack the Curse" setting out on foot in 2012 from spring training facilities in Mesa, Arizona, to Wrigley Field. They brought along a goat named Wrigley whom they believed could break the Curse of the Billy Goat upon arrival at Wrigley Field.

It is Sam Sianis, nephew of Billy Sianis, who says that the Curse of the Billy Goat can be dispelled only by the Chicago Cubs organization showing a sincere fondness for goats, allowing them into Wrigley Field because they genuinely want to and not simply for publicity reasons.

The Curse of the Billy Goat remains where it started, in the hands of the Sianis family and a chosen goat, probably named Murphy. It is their call.

William Sianis and Billy Goat Murphy

WRIGLEY ROOFTOPS

Since 1914, rooftops of nearby flat roofed apartment buildings in Wrigleyville around Wrigley Field found people sitting in folding chairs watching the Cubs play and other events going on at Wrigley Field. Folks even watched the games and events from porches and windows. All these activities were viewed FREE. Free, that is, until 1980 when formal seating structures began to appear and building owners began charging admission. The Cubs management did not take lightly to this free viewing as they saw it an "unreasonable encroachment."

In 2002, the Cubs organization filed a lawsuit against the different facilities for copyright infringement: since operators charged admission to use their amenities and sell licenses to view Major League Baseball, the Cubs claimed that their facilities were illegally using a copyrighted game and sued for royalties. In 2004, 11 of the 13 roofs settled with the club out of court, agreeing to pay 17% of gross revenue in exchange for official endorsement. The city began investigating the structural integrity of the roofs, issuing citations to those in danger of collapse. Many of the facilities began to feature seating structures: some with bleachers, some with chair seats, and one steel-girder viewing venue featured a double deck of chairs.

The Cubs finally endorsed Wrigley Rooftops "Official Rooftop Partners" on their website. The agreement is in force until 2023.

A LITTLE TRIVIA

What do Harvard University, Yale University, Cornell University, Columbia University, University of Pennsylvania, Princeton University, Brown University, Dartmouth College, and Wrigley Field have in common? They all have Parthenocissus tricuspidata, commonly known as Boston ivy, growing on their brick walls.

How did those northeast colleges become known as the Ivy League schools? Covered with Parthenocissus tricuspidata, commonly known as Boston ivy, the sobriquet "Ivy League" was a natural.

Why is the outfield brick wall at Wrigley Field covered with Parthenocissus tricuspidata, commonly known as Boston ivy? In 1937 when the stadium was modernized, owner P. K. Wrigley thought a sturdy vine covering the wall would protect the hard brick and Parthenocissus tricuspidata, commonly known as Boston ivy, has done that. The so-covered wall created rules about balls hit into it: if the ball is lost in the ivy, the outfielder must raise his hands signaling to the umpire he cannot find the ball; the umpire can then grant the ground double rule. If the outfielder makes an attempt to retrieve the ball from the ivy, the rule cannot be granted.

Who was the only player whose ball ever hit the Wrigley Field scoreboard? Sam Sneed in 1950 when he teed off from home plate and hit it with his golf ball.

And, will there be a brick wall covered with Parthenocissus tricuspitata, commonly known as Boston ivy, at Purnell Wrigley Field in Waterville, Maine? Of course there will.

Tony Campana cushioned by Wrigley Field ivy

WHY FENWAY? WHY RED SOX?

"It's in the Fenway section of Boston, isn't it? Then call it Fenway Park."
—John I. Taylor

Originally called the Red Stockings, the name came with the Cincinnati Red Stockings when they came to Boston in 1871, having left Cincinnati due to slumping attendance. The National League was formed in 1876 and the Boston Red Stockings became a charter member. Over the years, the Red Stockings became known as "The Red Caps," the "Beaneaters," the "Doves," the "Pilgrims," and by 1912, they became the "Braves," eventually moving to Milwaukee in 1953, and on to Atlanta in 1966.

In 1901, Ben Johnson formed the American League to compete with the National League and the new Boston club was formed. The team wore blue stockings and did not have an official name. They were simply known as "the Bostons" or the "Boston Baseball club." On December 18, 1907, new owner John I. Taylor announced that "beginning in the 1908 season, the team would start wearing white uniforms with bright red stockings for home games and as a result would be officially known as the Red Socks."

The Green Monster

WHY FENWAY? WHY RED SOX?

April 20, 1914, The Boston Red Sox play their first game in their new park. They were playing the New York Highlanders who became the Yankees the next year. Eleven innings and the Sox beat the Highlanders 7 - 6.

The Green Monster was originally tin and wasn't green for its first 35 years. It was painted green in 1947 and twenty years after that, replaced with hard plastic. There is debate as to the number of dents in it. The Boston Globe estimated 211,044 in a 2014 report. An imaging software company begged to differ and gave their estimate at 164,430. It's your call.

ANOTHER CURSE BECOMES A LEGEND

The Curse of the Bambino

Unlike Chicago Cubs Wrigley Field fans who know they have been under the Curse of the Billy Goat since 1945, Boston Red Sox fans didn't know they were under a curse until suggested by George Vecsey of the New York Times who wrote about the 1986 World Series games between the New York Mets and that the Boston Red Sox were a sure win. The tide had finally turned in their favor thanks to an error in Game 6 forcing Game 7 which they lost. The columnist titled his article "Babe Ruth Curse Strikes Again," followed by "All the ghosts and demons and curses of the past 68 years continued to haunt the Boston Red Sox last night." Many had felt that the curse began with the sale of Ruth from the Red Sox to the New York Yankees.

February 6, 1895. George Herman Ruth Jr. is born to a poor Catholic family in a rundown part of Baltimore. Getting into trouble early on, at age 7 his parents sent him to St. Mary's Industrial School for Boys, a Catholic orphanage and reformatory. It was his home for 12 years. Monk Brother Matthias was a father figure to Ruth. He and other monks suggested he play baseball. He immediately showed skills as a strong hitter and pitcher. Jack Dunn, owner of the Baltimore Orioles, which was at the time part of the farm league that groomed players for the Boston Red Sox, noticed Ruth and offered him a contract to play for the Orioles. Ruth was 19 and had to have a legal guardian sign the contract in order to play professionally. Dunn became that guardian. On February 14, 1914, George Herman Ruth Jr. signed with the Baltimore Orioles. Teammates jokingly called him "Dunn's new babe." He was now Babe Ruth.

July 11, 1914. Babe Ruth made his Major League debut with the Boston Red Sox as their pitcher. During the years between 1914 and 1919, he became a successful left-handed pitcher winning 65 games. During that same period, the Red Sox won three World Series. However, 1919 was not a good year for the Red Sox even with Babe hitting 29 home runs.

December 26, 1919. Harry Freeze, new owner of the Boston Red Sox, was in debt and he sold Babe Ruth to the New York Yankees for $125,000. The Boston Red Sox did not win a World Series until 2004. They were close: in Game 6 of the 1986 World Series with the New York Mets, an error in the 6th inning forced Game 7. George Vecsey of the *New York Times* wrote about the Sox winning Game 6 and redeeming their long drought. After Game 7 which they lost, his column was titled "Babe Ruth Curse Strikes Again." The curse: the sale of Babe Ruth to the New York Yankees.

April 18, 1923. The New York Yankees are in their new stadium. The Red Sox are there to face their nemesis. Babe Ruth hits a three-run homer in the four-run third inning. The Sox lose 4 - 1; Yankee Stadium is now known as "The House That Ruth Built." With Babe Ruth the Yankees went on to play in 37 World Series, winning 26 times. Babe Ruth went on to be among the first five players inducted into the Baseball Hall of Fame.

ANOTHER CURSE BECOMES A LEGEND

1990. Dan Shaughnessy of the Boston Globe published his book *The Curse of the Bambino* which became the catch phrase that continues to this day. The Red Sox went 84 years without a World Series win until 2004. Is the curse of the Bambino at Fenway Park finally lifted? Perhaps a young gifted player at Maine's Fenway in Oakland, Maine, will one day assure us it has.

Babe Ruth

Babe Ruth's last game

DEERFOOT OF THE DIAMOND

October 24, 1871 - December 24, 1913. Louis Francis Sockalexis, grandson of a Penobscot Indian chief, was born into the Penobscot Indian tribe on the Penobscot Reservation in Old Town, Maine. He grew up with dreams of fields in which to play baseball and his dreams came true.

Louis Francis Sockalexis became the first Native American to play professional baseball. He played outfield for the Cleveland Spiders from 1897-1899. The then racial slur "Indian" when he came on the field became a call of adoration and he was lovingly given the nickname "Deerfoot of the Diamond." In 1915, the Cleveland Spiders became the Cleveland Indians in his honor. He led the way for Native Americans Charlie Bender, John Meyers, Jim Thorpe, Bucky Dent, and Jacoby Ellsbury to play major league baseball.

Purnell Wrigley Field. Maine's Fenway. Cleveland Indian Louis Sockalexis. Firsts in baseball. Firsts in Maine.

Penobscot Nation native Louis Sockalexis--the reason for the Cleveland Spiders to change their name to the Indians.

JOHN WESLEY COOMBS

John Wesley Coombs, November 18, 1882 - April 15, 1957. Born in LeGrand, Iowa, Jack and his family moved to Kennebunk, Maine, when he was four, played baseball in high school, and ultimately enrolled in Colby College in 1902 where he majored in chemistry. He played baseball at Colby where he became known as "Iron Man Jack" for his side arm delivery and led Colby to several Maine collegiate championships where he played every position. He spent his summers playing semi-professional baseball. In Northampton, Massachusetts, where he caught the eye of Tom Mack, Connie Mack's brother, manager and part owner of the Philadelphia Athletics.

Although accepted at MIT for graduate work, Colby Jack signed up with Tom Mack in 1905 to play for the Athletics after he graduated from Colby in 1906. He made a successful major league debut on July 5, 1906, pitching a seven-hit shutout defeating the Washington Senators 3-0. July and August were not impressive. However, September 1, starting against Boston in what was to be a double header, he turned it into a single 4-hour-27-minute 24-inning contest in which he and the Boston rookie Joe Harris went the distance. Colby Jack won the game 4-1.

Intervening years were successful, including the Athletics' first World Series win in 1910 against the Chicago Cubs. With only two pitchers and no relief pitchers and no closers, Connie Mack alternated Chief Bender and Colby Jack Coombs the entire series. Colby Jack won three of the four games.

Retiring from professional ball in 1920, and coaching at several colleges in the intervening years, in 1929, he started coaching at Duke University and coached there for 23 years, retiring in 1953. It was at Duke where he met and mentored John Winkin. Duke and Colby have honored John Wesley Coombs – "Colby Jack" – with baseball fields bearing the Coombs name.

John Wesley Coombs
Colby baseball star who turned pro.
He played for Connie Mack.

A MAINE YANKEE

Clyde Leroy Sukeforth. November 30, 1901 - September 3, 2000. "Sukey" was a consummate Maine Yankee: reticent, practical, resourceful, loyal, independent, humble, discourse often understated with a wry Maine sense of humor.

Sukeforth was born in Washington, Maine, a village of about 1,000 people, inland but not too far from the coast, went to Georgetown University for two years, followed by a year in the New England League and in 1926 signed as a catcher by the Cincinnati Reds. Two years later, a bird hunting accident left him with partial sight in his right eye. In 1932, he was traded to the Brooklyn Dodgers. He appeared in 486 games overall and in parts of ten big-league seasons during 1926-1934 and in 1945 as a fill-in for players serving in the military during World War II.

Sukey managed the Brooklyn farm system from 1937-1942 and was promoted to the Dodger coaching staff in 1943. In 1945, when the major league teams had an unwritten policy to ignore black players, Sukeforth, Dodger's President Branch Rickey's collaborator and confidant, was assigned by Rickey to scout Jackie Robinson at a Negro league game in Chicago before bringing him back for an historic meeting in Branch Rickey's Brooklyn office.

Sukeforth: "When Jack came out on the field, I called him over and introduced myself and told him who sent me. He was amazed. He said: 'Why is Mr. Rickey interested in me?' I told him: 'I just work here. I have no authority to answer that question, but I can assure you there's a lot of interest in you in Brooklyn.'" (NY Times, Dave Anderson, 9/6/2000)

At that time Rickey was forming a Brooklyn Brown Dodgers team to play in a new black league. On the morning of August 23, 1945, Sukeforth ushered Robinson into Rickey's office. "We walked in and I said, 'Mr. Rickey, here is Jack Roosevelt Robinson,' and Mr. Rickey said, 'Jack, all my life I've been looking for a great colored ballplayer and I have reason to believe you might be that man.' That's when Jack realized Mr. Rickey was talking about the Dodgers, not the Brown Dodgers."

Sukeforth turned down opportunities to manage the Dodgers and the Pittsburgh Pirates, not wanting to give up his coaching position. He retired from coaching in 1957 but continued to be a scout and occasional Minor League manager for the Pirates and the Atlanta Braves. He continued to scout off and on until his 72nd year when he repaired to his beloved Maine to enjoy the rest of his life. "Times change, but I don't."

In 2013, in the sports film "42" about Robinson's entry into Major League baseball, Sukeforth was depicted in a few scenes by actor Toby Huss. In one of the movie's last scenes, Clyde Sukeforth, wearing uniform #40, is shown as the Dodgers' third base coach congratulating Robinson on hitting a home run.

"I get a lot of credit I don't deserve. I treated Robinson just like any other human being. See, coming from Maine, I never thought about color. I don't feel I did anything special. I was just there." In 1995, he told a reporter for the *Rockland Courier-Gazette* – "I just like the game and atmosphere. I felt at home in the ball park. ...I've made a living doing what I want to do. Baseball has been my life and it's been a great life." Yes. A great life for Maine Yankee Clyde Leroy Sukeforth. Clyde was great friends with John Winkin. The baseball coach often would call Clyde to discuss strategy of the game.

Jackie Robinson and Clyde Sukeforth before a game. Clyde, from Maine, was a former pro player, manager and scout. He signed Jackie to play for the Brooklyn Dodgers.

DR. JOHN W. WINKIN JR., Ed.D. JULY 24, 1919 - JULY 19, 2014

Dr. Winkin was not a native son. He was born in Englewood, New Jersey, went to Duke University for undergraduate work where he played center field baseball for head coach Colby Jack Coombs. Being 5 foot 6 inches didn't bother him – he played basketball and soccer as well. Throughout college, Colby Jack suggested John pursue a coaching career.

Upon graduating from Duke in 1941 with a bachelors degree in education, John joined the Navy, serving aboard the USS *McCall*, a destroyer assigned to protect the aircraft carrier USS *Enterprise*. After delivering Marines to Wake Island, the fleet was returning to port at Pearl Harbor on the evening of December 6, 1941. Hazardous weather prevented the McCall from returning to its berth beside the USS Arizona. The next morning, John Winkin and his crew mates watched the entire attack on Pearl Harbor unfold from the decks of the McCall in waters outside the harbor.

Returning to New Jersey after the war, he joined McFadden Publication in 1946 as a writer and founding editor of *Sport Magazine*. His reporting and interviewing work for the magazine led to a broadcasting position with the New York Yankees where he hosted the first pre-game TV show with Mel Allen and Curt Gowdy. He became friends with Joe DiMaggio and wore #5 at his college coaching in honor of Joe. His first coaching job was manager of the American Legion baseball team in Englewood. In 1949, the Superintendent of Schools of Englwood engaged him as football and baseball coach and history teacher.

His parents – his mother was a physician and his father a linguistics professor at Columbia University – were not happy about his coaching and to placate them, he earned his Master's and

DR. JOHN W. WINKIN JR., EdD. JULY 24, 1919 - JULY 19, 2014

Doctorate in education at Columbia University. His doctoral thesis was on the statistical probabilities of the double play.

In 1954, Colby Jack Coombs recommended Winkin to his alma mater, Colby College, and he spent the next 20 years as baseball coach and athletic director. As Athletic Director, John hired Dick Whitmore as basketball coach. Harold Alfond's long-time friend John "Swisher" Mitchell served as assistant basketball coach for 44 years. It was during that legendary time that John Winkin also became a trusted friend of Harold Alfond. The Colby coaching ended in 1974 and he moved on to the University of Maine as head baseball coach. He remained there until 1966 with a career coaching record of 642-430-3.

He continued coaching at Husson College in Bangor where he ended his career, the 44th collegiate baseball coach to reach 1000 career victories. He suffered a stroke December 10, 1997, and officially stepped down as head coach at the end of the 2008 season. While at Husson, he compiled an overall record of 100-74-8.

Dr. John Winkin died on July 18, 2014. Although he was "from away" as we say in Maine about anyone not born here, Dr. Winkin and Maine baseball are synonymous. We can overlook and call him ours.

FERGIE JENKINS

"One of the best pitchers in baseball, ever," Leo Durocher said of Fergie Jenkins.

Ferguson "Fergie" Jenkins. December 13, 1942, Chatham-Kent, Canada. Although he signed with the Philadelphia Phillies in 1962, he made his mark with the Chicago Cubs shortly thereafter. After five years in the bullpen, in 1967 he became a starting pitcher with 20 wins which included 236 strikeouts. He tied for second place for the Cy Young Award. The following year, again winning 20 games, he struck out 260. In a span of five years, he threw 97 complete games.

Fergie's best single game was pitched in the 1967 All-Star game when he struck out six American League top sluggers: Harmon Killebrew, Tony Conigliaro, Mickey Mantle, Jim Fregosi, Rod Carew and Tony Oliva.

In 1971, he was the National League Cy Young Award winner, the first Cubs pitcher and the first Canadian to ever win the award. He was inducted into the Canadian Baseball Hall of Fame in 1987 and into the National Baseball Hall of Fame in 1991.

Ferguson Jenkins – Fergie – although he has had a stunning career as a baseball pitcher, his grace as a player exemplifies what baseball is about. We are privileged to have him serve as Honorary Chair of Purnell Wrigley Field.

HOF Cubs pitcher Fergie Jenkins visits the Alfond Youth Center.
Here he is playing sandlot baseball with the kids in 2015.

WHO IS FRAN PURNELL?

Mayoral Proclamation

Whereas for over forty years Fran Purnell organized, coached and managed the Waterville Little League program. Fran's entire spring, summer nights and weekends were dedicated to building the baseball program to a level of excellence. Thousands of children learned the fundamentals of the game while Fran stressed sportsmanship and the importance of respect on and off the field.

Whereas Fran Purnell and his volunteers renovated the field on Mathews avenue. He overhauled the infield and outfield, backstop, dugouts and snack shacks, installed a flag pole, PA system, remote score board and field lights, built a storage area and press box and raised the pitcher's mound to specifications.

Whereas In honor of Fran's work and dedication the Matthews Field in Waterville was renamed the Purnell Little League Field.

Whereas In 1990 Fran started the "Challenger Division" so that children and adults with disabilities could flourish in the game. After twenty-six years Fran still plays an active role each and every Friday evening coaching and supporting the program at Purnell Field.

Whereas In gratitude and in honor of Fran's unselfish commitment to the youth and families, the City of Waterville along with the Alfond Youth Center will renovate the Purnell Field to become a licensed Major League Baseball Turf field with an ADA surface to be called the PURNELL WRIGLEY FIELD.

Whereas the City of Waterville is truly grateful for the important work of Fran Purnell, his family and the many volunteers, for improving the quality of life for so many of the city's residents;

Now therefore, I, Nicholas Isgro, Mayor of Waterville, on behalf of the City Council, do hereby recognize April 23, 2016, in honor of Fran "Mr. Baseball" Purnell as the official FRAN PURNELL DAY during the opening ceremony of the 2016 Baseball season.

In Witness Whereof, I do hereby set my hands and seal this 23rd day of April, Two thousand and sixteen.

Nicholas Isgro, Mayor

All Star former Cubs relief pitcher Lee Smith pays tribute to Fran Purnell during the groundbreaking ceremony.

Thirty years ago, a little girl wanted to play baseball but there were no girl teams. Her father, volunteer coach Fran Purnell, thought it unfair and decided to find a way for his daughter to play, albeit on a boys team. With hair tucked into her hat, 11-year-old Deb Purnell (now Poulin) could pass as a boy. Her team members knew she was a girl but she had a strong arm, steady fielding, and a powerful swing which was just what they needed on their team. The away teams could not decide if Deb was a boy or a girl and word traveled throughout Central Maine that perhaps a girl – the first – was playing Little League Baseball. She played second base the whole season and led her team into the playoff. She broke through an all-boys sport which led to a league change.

Who is Fran Purnell? That is Fran Purnell.

A boy in a wheel chair, Red Sox baseball cap on backwards, was watching a ball game at Purnell Field outside the fence and wishing he could play. Fran Purnell noticed the boy, went over to him, introduced himself, and asked if he liked watching the game. The boy nodded and continued watching the game. The boy's mother told Fran that he would love to play. A restless night gave Fran a decision – he told his wife Joyce he was going to start a league for children with disabilities to play baseball. The Challenger program did just that: children and adults with disabilities could play baseball every Friday night. Purnell Field became theirs with Fran Purnell coaching. Sadly, the boy watching from his wheelchair outside the fence died. However, he played baseball for ten years and at his request, he was buried in his baseball uniform. His team played a game in his honor. On September 6, 2016, the Challengers were special guests at the dedication of the Purnell

Wrigley Field to share in the festivities honoring their mentor, Fran Purnell, and to remember their friend who made it possible for them to be on the playing side of the fence.

Who is Fran Purnell? That is Fran Purnell.

Lee Smith with the Challenger players

When complete, Purnell Wrigley Field in Waterville will join Maine's Fenway at Camp Tracy in Oakland as the only two turf fields in the country licensed by Major League Baseball. Like Fenway Park with its iconic Monster Wall at Maine's Fenway, Wrigley Field's iconic Boston ivy (Parthenocissus tricuspidata) will be covering the walls at Purnell Wrigley Field. Harold Alfond and Fran Purnell are legends in their love of baseball and the need to provide children a place where they can play ball. Having baseball fields named in their honor is perfect recognition of the dedication and generosity to the game.

Lee Smith who relief pitched for the Chicago Cubs for eight years and stood in for Honorary Chair Ferguson Jenkins at the dedication of Purnell Wrigley Field, said, "You're going to spoil the kids, man. We didn't have fields like this when we played." Further, "This reminds me of home. I threw my first pitch in the Majors at Wrigley Field in 1980." There will be others reminiscing about throwing their first pitch at home at Wrigley Field, Purnell Wrigley Field, that is.

BACK TO THE BEGINNING

There were many baseball years before Purnell Wrigley Field. In 1950, Harold Alfond was interested in beginning a baseball program for kids and reached out to his friends John Winkin and John Mitchell to coach and manage a program he would fund. The program would be organized under the Waterville Boys Club. The first fields were developed on a country road along the Messalonskee Stream and at Lockwood Park across from the Hathaway shirt factory. The Boys Club ran the program until the late 60s. Included in the program was Fran Purnell's nine-year-old son Chris. Wanting to watch his son pay baseball, Fran gave up his traveling job for local work and within a short time was recruited to coach, eventually taking over the program and developing a volunteer group to work with him

Endless hours were spent helping the program and maintaining the fields. Then, in the mid-60s, the Lockwood Little League field was taken away from the organization. The Waterville City Councilors promised to replace Lockwood Field with a new field but never did. Thus, Fran and his volunteer crew took it upon themselves to find a replacement field. The Boys Club did not have the funds to continue the Little League operation so Fran asked Boys Club Director Mike Gallagher if he could take over the program. Mike liked the idea; thus, Fran and his volunteers started the Little League Booster Organization which ran for 48 years.

On Mathews Avenue adjacent to the Averill grammar school was an open lot used by kids in the area as a play field, a play field just right for a Little League field. Fran and his volunteers Mike and Laurie White, Bruce and Bev Charrer, Russel Vince, and Arthur "Tar" Bizzier, some of whom had children in the Little League program, started renovating the field. The first new addition, a backstop built with three telephone poles and chicken wire, was placed in the far corner of the field. During the games, an all-purpose army tent served as the concession stand which was eventually replaced by a wooden stand. There was an ice skating rink near the school and an ice skating program which the volunteers stopped. A 12' x 24' equipment building at that site was left vacant. Fran and his team obtained permission to use it. Soon, fences were put in along with dugouts. New lights were installed. Renovations continued for many years. Fran made it possible for girls to play in Little League and he started the Challenger program for children with disabilities to play and made the field available to them every Friday night.

Additions were made to the volunteer crew, including Roland Boucher and Buster and Ellen Huggins who ran the finances of the program and the concession stand. In 1985, at the annual Little League dinner, Mayor Tom Nale announced to the two hundred guests that the Matthews Avenue field would henceforth be known as Purnell Field.

In the winter of 2014, Fran asked Ken Walsh, CEO of the Alfond Youth Center, if he had interest in taking over the program as he was ready to retire from his years of volunteer services and thought the Boys & Girls Club and YMCA would be the right fit to continue the efforts to serve the kids. Ken agreed immediately; he was honored. The Alfond Youth Center would take over what Fran had started so many years ago. Although several coaches felt it not a good idea, Fran did not waiver in his decision.

Harold Alfond had offered to contribute to establishing the replica of Fenway Park at Camp Tracy but Ken felt it was time to give back to Harold for his generosity. Ken raised the funds to establish the Harold Alfond Fenway Park. With the newly licensed replica Wrigley Field being considered to be built at the Purnell Field location, as well as other locations, Purnell Field would become home to Wrigley Field. Ken felt Fran Purnell's years of service to the community, volunteering 45 years of his time so children could play baseball, should be recognized as was Harold Alfond. He made it official that Fran Purnell would be honored by naming the replicated Wrigley Field the Purnell Wrigley Field.

With the location in place, fundraising began. Merchants supported the effort. The Waterville Public Works and Park & Recreation Department led by Matt Skehans and Mike Folsom provided the needed equipment for the demolition of the site structure; Fran's son Kevin provided the plumbing for the concession stand; Dave Leach took on the lighting project; Central Maine Power moved telephone light poles; Waterville Public Works worked on the flag pole memorial park and parking. This grass roots effort saved the project $600,000 of the $1.4 million cost. $850,000 was raised in eight months! An additional $500,000 came from generous contributions from the Harold Alfond Foundation, NET Sports Turf, Major League Baseball Tomorrow Fund (Major League Baseball is partnered with The Boys Club and Girls Club in generously supporting urban baseball and softball for boys and girls), Borman Foundation, and Central Maine Motors.

We have been back to the beginning and now look to the future. In 2017, the Cal Ripken New England Regional Championship games will be played at Wrigley and Fenway. The Alfond Youth Center is teaming up with Special Olympics to host the first Challenger tournament in the fall. Children will play baseball all summer and will be challenged to hit a home run over the Green Monster Wall at Maine's Fenway and the Wall covered with Boston ivy at Purnell Wrigley Field.

NO CURSE NO MORE

November 3, 2016. 12:47a.m. Cleveland time. The Chicago Cubs beat the Cleveland Indians in the World Series, a win for the Cubs for first time in 108 years. Waterville, Maine, is holding dear to that moment when time stood still with a 30' wide by 15' high scoreboard in dead center field identical to the Chicago Cubs scoreboard where the clock stopped at 12:47 a.m. Underneath the clock in script here as there reads "Chicago Cubs World Champions."

Summer 2017. At Purnell Wrigley Field in Waterville, 1,160 miles from Chicago Cubs Wrigley Field, championship baseball will be played by 120 players representing the New England states. The teams will compete in their World Series for the Cal Ripken championships. They will test the turf field and be part of the magic of Purnell Wrigley Field. On hand for the opening ceremony and to witness that magic will be Ferguson Jenkins, Hall of Fame Chicago Cubs pitcher and Honorary Chair of Purnell Wrigley Field, and other Major League Baseball players. The day will be pure baseball with the smell of hot dogs and popcorn and kids everywhere with pens and baseballs asking for autographs to commemorate the day. Those kids will be the new Cubs fans at Purnell Wrigley Field in Waterville, 1160 miles from Chicago Wrigley Field.

Dreams do come true if "you go the distance" and "if you build it, they will come."

All proceeds from the sale of *Fields of Dreams* will be placed in an endowment to provide for the maintenance of Purnell Wrigley Field.

About the Authors

KENNETH A. WALSH

Ken was born in Brooklyn, New York, and at the age of 12 moved with his parents and six siblings to Amenia, a small town upstate. It was in Amenia playing sand lot baseball that his passion for baseball developed. *The Depot Hill Gang* (North Country Press, 2014) tells about those sand lot games and stories of his youth and friends coming of age.

Upon graduating from State University of New York in January 1985, he accepted the position as Director of the Boys & Girls Clubs of New Rochelle, New York. In 1992, he moved to Waterville, Maine, to lead the Waterville Area Boys & Girls Clubs as their Executive Director. It was during this time that Ken developed a unique friendship with philanthropist and minority Red Sox owner Harold Alfond who provided Ken with opportunities to develop what ultimately became the Alfond Youth Center. It was Ken's personal pleasure to thank Mr. Alfond for his generosities by naming the Major League Baseball Fenway Park replica at YMCA summer Camp Tracy the Harold Alfond Fenway Park.

With the new project of building Purnell Wrigley Field, another licensed replica Major League Baseball Park in the Waterville area, the excitement intensified; it is the same year the Cubs won the World Series in 108 years. They are honored to recognize Fran Purnell by naming the field for him. Fran has given forty-eight years of volunteer service to the game which included making sure children with special needs were able to play. He is a testament to the success of people who get behind a cause.

Ken's passion for baseball continues. At the age of 55, he came out of "retirement" and decided to play ball again. He had a successful season playing in the Central Maine Men's Wooden Bat Baseball League starting at second base and has challenged himself to come back next season batting left handed.

Co-author Barbara "Bubbe" Jolovitz and Ken also wrote *Behold the Turtle* which documented the founding and growth of Camp Tracy. Bubbe is part of Ken's family and feels very lucky to have her be part of his life as she inspires others in her Bubbe's world.

Ken lives in Vassalboro, Maine, with his wife Suzanne, a die-hard Red Sox fan, and their nine-year-old son Sean who announced this year he favors the Yankees which has created interesting dinner table conversations. Their six-year-old daughter Kate, on the other hand, could care less.

BARBARA ROGERS JOLOVITZ

In her 76th year, totally new to the world of book writing, Barbara wrote *Reminiscences and Recipes* (North Country Press, 2012) which was entered in the 2013 Maine Literary Awards in the "John N. Cole Award for Maine-Themed nonfiction." Since then, she has collaborated with Ken Walsh, CEO of the Alfond Youth Center in Waterville, Maine, on *Behold the Turtle* (North Country Press, 2014). *Turtle* is the history of YMCA Camp Tracy, founded by her late husband Lester and two other Waterville men, and is written in the voice of the turtle. *A Singular Peluche* (North Country Press, 2014) is a fantasy about a teddy bear found in a toy bin waiting to be picked up and loved.

And now, *Fields of Dreams*. Ken and Barbara wanted to tell the tales of the Chicago Cubs and the Boston Red Sox and how they impacted baseball in Waterville as Purnell Wrigley Field and Maine's Fenway. History holds the tales which they have repeated in small measure.

Barbara's family includes her children, Karl and Deborah; grandsons Ben, Will and Nicky, and what Ken calls her Bubbe World, loving caring people for whom she has become their Bubbe, their grandmother.

www.ingramcontent.com/pod-product-compliance
Lightning Source LLC
Chambersburg PA
CBHW041637040426
42449CB00020B/3486